BIBLE NEWS PROPHECY

 7  11  32

In This Issue:

2 **From the Editor: Prophetic Ramifications of the Seventh Day of Unleavened Bread**
The children of Israel crossed the Red Sea on the 7th Day of Unleavened Bread. Could the last day of unleavened bread have any prophetic lessons for Christians today?

3 **Questions and Answers About Prophecy** An update to questions and answers put together by the old Ambassador College.

7 **The Third Commandment** Do words matter?

11 **Study the Bible Course Lesson 15: What is 'Hell'?** Most in the world greatly misunderstand this subject.

26 **What Does Pentecost Mean to You?** Can understanding Pentecost help correct one of the most universally believed false doctrine in the world's 'Christianity'?

29 **The Origins of Astrology** The origins are not biblical, nor have most people been born under the sign astrologers claim.

32 **Youth and Singles** Q&A This article answers questions some teens and singles have wondered about.

Back Cover: Internet and Radio This shows where people can find the messages from the *Continuing* Church of God.

About the Front Cover: Thousands of years ago, the children of Israel crossed the Red Sea on the 7th Day of Unleavened Bread. May there be ramifications in the 21st century? Cover developed for the Continuing Church of God.

Bible News Prophecy magazine is published by the *Continuing* Church of God, 1036 W. Grand Avenue, Grover Beach, CA, 93433. http://www.ccog.org

©2019 *Continuing* Church of God. Printed in the U.S.A. All rights reserved.

Reproduction in whole or in part without written permission is prohibited. We do respect your privacy and we do not rent, trade, or sell our mailing list. If you do not want to receive this magazine, simply contact our Grover Beach office. Scripture references are from the New King James Version (©Thomas Nelson, Inc., Publishers, used by permission or for 20th century articles the KJV) unless otherwise noted.

Bible News Prophecy — SUPPORTED BY YOUR CONTRIBUTIONS

Bible News Prophecy has no subscription or newsstand price. This magazine is provided free of charge by the Continuing Church of God. It is made possible by the voluntary, freely given tithes and offerings of the membership of the Church and others who have elected to support the work of the Church. Contributions are gratefully welcomed and are tax-deductible in the U.S. Those who wish to voluntarily aid and support this worldwide Work of God are gladly welcomed as co-workers in this major effort to preach and publish the gospel to all nations. Contributions should be sent to: Continuing Church of God, 1036 W. Grand Avenue, Grover Beach, CA, 93433.

Editor in Chief: Bob Thiel

Copy/Proofing Editor: Joyce Thiel

Proofreader: John Hickey;
SBC Course Assister: Shirley Gestro.

Photos: All photos come from the Thiel family or public domain sources such as Wikipedia, Pixabay, or certain governments (unless specific attribution is given).

Layout and Design:
James Erwin EStoque

April - June 2019

FROM THE EDITOR IN CHIEF: BOB THIEL

PROPHETIC RAMIFICATIONS OF THE SEVENTH DAY OF UNLEAVENED BREAD

Could the last day of unleavened bread have any prophetic lessons for Christians today?

To try to answer that, let's first go to the Book of Leviticus:

> 5 On the fourteenth day of the first month at twilight is the Lord's Passover. 6 And on the fifteenth day of the same month is the Feast of Unleavened Bread to the Lord; seven days you must eat unleavened bread.
>
> 7 On the first day you shall have a holy convocation; you shall do no customary work on it. 8 But you shall offer an offering made by fire to the Lord for seven days. The seventh day shall be a holy convocation; you shall do no customary work on it.' (Leviticus 23:5-8)

Other than the number seven being a number that God has used to signal completion, was there anything special about the Seventh day of Unleavened Bread?

Well, from Leviticus 23, we see it is a Sabbath day—you do not do normal work, plus have a holy convocation (like attending church services). The Seventh day of Unleavened Bread equates to the 21st day of the month of Nisan/Abib (both names are used in the Bible for the first month of the year per Exodus 13:4 and Esther 3:7).

In the New Testament, consider that Jude warned that:

> 4 For certain men have crept in unnoticed, who long ago were marked out for this condemnation, ungodly men who turn the grace of our God into licentiousness and deny the only Lord God and our Lord Jesus Christ. (Jude 4)

This is interesting because in the next verse he ties this problem with deliverance (from Egypt) during the Days of Unleavened Bread (which should be kept as an annual reminder of sin and deliverance, Exodus 13:3-10, 1 Corinthians 5:8):

> 5 But I want to remind you, though you once knew this, that the Lord, having saved the people out of the land of Egypt, afterward destroyed those who did not believe. (Jude 5)

In like manner, just because of the sacrifice of Jesus "God had passed over the sins that were previously committed" (Romans 3:25), He may afterward destroy "those who did not believe."

Now, understand that it was on the 21st of Nisan/Abib, the Seventh (the last) Day of Unleavened Bread, God had the Red Sea parted (Exodus 14:20-21). God called for the children of Israel to cross on dry land under the cloud (Exodus 14:20-22,29), where they were symbolically baptized (1 Corinthians 10:1-2). They endured their fleeing with their enemies behind them and the waters stopped on both sides of them.

During the daylight hours of the 21st, the Egyptian army pursued them and was destroyed (Exodus 14:23-28).

Understand that it was on the Seventh Day of Unleavened bread that the Hebrews crossed the Red Sea and the army of Egypt was destroyed. The Seventh, the last, Day of Unleavened Bread pictures fully leaving the dead works of sin behind.

A Christian sequence of events starts from our acceptance of Jesus, repentance, and baptism (Acts 2:38-39). Christians endure to the end (Matthew 10:22) attaining to the first resurrection (Revelation 20:6) to be called to the marriage supper of the Lamb (Revelation 19:9).

The crossing of the Red Sea may have other lessons for Philadelphian Christians. As they flee to a place in the wilderness just prior to the start of the Great

Tribulation, it will take some time to get there and Satan will be angry with them (Revelation 12:13-16).

During the time the Philadelphian Christians are being protected (Revelation 3:7-13), bad things will be happening in the world around them (Revelation 12:14-17). They will often need to "walk by faith, not by sight" (2 Corinthians 5:7).

Furthermore, the New Testament also seemingly shows a fulfillment of the destruction of Pharaoh's army in the destruction of the world's armies who will fight against the returning Jesus (Revelation 19:19-21).

The Seventh Day of Unleavened Bread helps picture the end of the world's systems and getting closer to the emergence of the Kingdom of God.

In the Continuing Church of God, it is one of the biblical Holy Days we keep. It has lessons for us today.

Questions & Answers - About Prophecy

Edited by Bob Thiel

When it was around, the staff of the old Ambassador College put together some questions and answers about prophecy. This article is basically an update of some of them with some additional scriptures and clarifications as many still wonder about many of these same matters today.

Q. There are two accounts of the second coming in the New Testament. The first account says Jesus will come 'as a thief in the night,' and in the second account He will 'come in the clouds of glory, and every eye shall see Him.' Now, which one (if any) can we believe?

A. Revelation 1:7 ("Behold he is coming with the clouds, and every eye will see him") refers to the manner of Christ's coming. The statement that "the day of the Lord will come like a thief in the night" (1 Thessalonian 5:2; 2 Peter. 3:10) refers to the time of His coming. He will arrive like a thief — at a time few expect. The context shows this:

> 1 But concerning the times and the seasons, brethren, you have no need that I should write to you. 2 For you yourselves know perfectly that the day of the Lord so comes as a thief in the night. (1 Thessalonians 5:1-2)

There is no contradiction between these two concepts: Christ will arrive in a dramatic, obvious manner (Matt. 24:29-31), but the time of this coming is known only to God the Father (Matt. 24:36) and it will take many by surprise just like a thief in the night.

Q. Is prophecy conditional in certain instances?

Buildings once part of Ambassador College

Yes, certain parts of the prophetic writings are conditional, although some prophecies such as those predicting Christ's second coming and the utopian millennial reign are unconditional.

God gives people a choice; if we repent, He will have mercy on us. Leviticus 26 illustrates this principle. It enumerates the blessings and curses prophesied to come upon ancient Israel according to whether or not they kept the covenant God made with them.

The same concept is found in Deuteronomy 29 and 30:

> 1 "Now it shall come to pass, when all these things come upon you, the blessing and the curse which I have set before you, and you call them to mind among all the nations where the Lord your God drives you, 2 and you return to the Lord your God and obey His voice, according to all that I command you today, you and your children, with all your heart and with all your soul, 3 that the Lord your God will bring you back from captivity, and have compassion on you, and gather you again from all the nations

where the Lord your God has scattered you. 4 If any of you are driven out to the farthest parts under heaven, from there the Lord your God will gather you, and from there He will bring you. 5 Then the Lord your God will bring you to the land which your fathers possessed, and you shall possess it. He will prosper you and multiply you more than your fathers. 6 And the Lord your God will circumcise your heart and the heart of your descendants, to love the Lord your God with all your heart and with all your soul, that you may live.

7 "Also the Lord your God will put all these curses on your enemies and on those who hate you, who persecuted you. 8 And you will again obey the voice of the Lord and do all His commandments which I command you today. 9 The Lord your God will make you abound in all the work of your hand, in the fruit of your body, in the increase of your livestock, and in the produce of your land for good. For the Lord will again rejoice over you for good as He rejoiced over your fathers, 10 if you obey the voice of the Lord your God, to keep His commandments and His statutes which are written in this Book of the Law, and if you turn to the Lord your God with all your heart and with all your soul. (Deuteronomy 30:1-10)

The entire book of Jonah is an account of how God sent one of His prophets to the ancient city of Nineveh to warn them of their impending doom if they did not mend their ways. They accepted the warning:

5 So the people of Nineveh believed God, proclaimed a fast, and put on sackcloth, from the greatest to the least of them. (Jonah 3:5)

Notice God's reaction:

10 Then God saw their works, that they turned from their evil way; and God relented from the disaster that He had said He would bring upon them, and He did not do it. (Jonah 3:10)

Another example of the outcome of prophecy being delayed by repentance is found in 2 Chronicles 32.

24 In those days Hezekiah was sick and near death, and he prayed to the Lord; and He spoke to him and gave him a sign. 25 But Hezekiah did not repay according to the favor shown him, for his heart was lifted up; therefore wrath was looming over him and over Judah and Jerusalem. (2 Chronicles 32:24-25)

Hezekiah repented:

26 Then Hezekiah humbled himself for the pride of his heart, he and the inhabitants of Jerusalem, so that the wrath of the Lord did not come upon them in the days of Hezekiah. (2 Chronicles 32:26)

We see when a nation or individual repents, God has mercy on them.

In some of your writings that deal with prophecy of the future, you seem to indicate a belief that the end of the age and Christ's return may occur seven to twenty years from now. Why?

There has been much speculation about the precise time of Jesus' return to this earth. World conditions would seem to indicate that we are living near the close of an age. Many of man's global problems seem to have reached the point of no return. Environmental destruction, the capacity for total war, rapid and continuing economic breakdown, and the moral and social problems of modern society amount to strong evidence that Christ must soon intervene to save man from himself (Matthew 24:22, Moffatt).

Early Christians seemed to believe that Jesus would return 6000 years after Adam and Eve were put out of the Garden of Eden. If we look at various genealogies, historical events, and biblical prophecies, we can get an approximation. Furthermore, when we look at the signs Jesus referred to in Matthew 24 and tie those in with certain prophecies in the Book of Daniel, we have an idea.

Though we do not know the date and hour (cf. Matthew 24:36), we will have a much better idea once certain events (e.g. Daniel 9:27, 11:31; Matthew 24:14-16) are fulfilled.

Q. In an article published by the old Worldwide Church of God titled, 'The God Family' the author

mentions God's 7,000-year plan for earth. Would you please explain what was meant by this?

A. Up until now God has allowed approximately 6,000 years for humanity to write the painful lesson of "doing its own thing" — going its own way without the revealed knowledge of its Creator.

A study of biblical chronology and other records indicates that Adam and Eve (our first parents) were created a bit less than 4,000 years before Christ (Genesis 5, 10; 1 Chronicles 1-9, Matthew 1; Luke 3).

And almost another 2,000 years have elapsed since the time of Christ's resurrection—totalling nearly 6,000 years of human civilization to date.

And the Bible tells us that shortly after the appearance of Christ on this earth again, a peaceful, utopian, 1,000-year reign begins on this planet (Revelation 20:1-10; Isaiah 11).

These two general spans of time (approximately 6,000 years of humanity's rule; approximately 1,000 years of God's rule) add up to a period of about 7,000 years.

Further, the 7,000-year concept comes from an analogy between the perfect weekly cycle (seven days) and the apparent 6,000 years allotted to mankind prior to the millennium.

We must realize that even though the saints will live and reign with Christ for 1,000 years (Revelation 20:4), there is still an unspecified period of time allowed after the millennium during which Satan will be loosed and the Great White Throne judgment will take place (Revelation 20:11-12). These spans of time are in addition to the 7,000-year period.

The main biblical indication of a 7000-year plan is the evidence provided by the millennium as a type of God's rest or Sabbath (compare Revelation 20 and Hebrews 4). If the millennium represents a "Sabbath," then it would be logically preceded by six similar 1,000-year "days." Jewish tradition says that the school of the prophet Elijah taught this and early writers associated with Christianity also elaborated on this.

2 Peter 3:8 provides a New Testament basis for setting the length of each millennial day: "... One day is with the Lord as [Greek: hos] a thousand years, and a thousand years as [hos] one day."

But we need to realize that even if we understand this as a literal statement regarding a 7,000-year plan, it may not be giving us a precise, measured duration.

Why not? Because the Greek term hos before numerals denotes "nearly," "about," "approximately." Compare its usage in Mark 5:13, "about two thousand"; Mark 8:9, "about four thousand"; John 6:19, "about five and twenty or thirty"; John 21:8, "as it were two hundred cubits"; Acts 13:18, 20; "about the time of forty years... about the space of four hundred and fifty years."

Plus, Jesus taught that the days would be shortened (Matthew 24:22), which either seems to mean that there will be less than 6,000 before the millennium or that if God allowed the world to go the way it was going without Jesus' return, humanity would have destroyed all life from the planet before the 7,000 years would be completed.

When we look at various world events, and behaviours (cf. 2 Timothy 3:1-5), in the light of biblical prophecies, it seems that world events are consistent (cf. Matthew 24) with the idea of the 6000 years coming close to an end and the return of Jesus to establish the 7th thousand years.

Q. In an article by David Jon Hill published by the old Worldwide Church of God titled, 'What the World Needs is Hope,' it was stated that God plans to expand His family for eternity by adding sons and daughters. Will God do this by spiritual creation as He created the angels, or is this given for us to know (1 Corinthians 2:9)?

A. The concept that God will continue to expand His family for eternity is a very logical inference drawn from a prophecy of Christ which states:

> 7 Of the increase of His government and peace There will be no end, (Isaiah 9:7)

Some have speculated that when we are immortal spirit beings, sons and daughters of God in His family, we will have a part in extending God's Kingdom throughout the universe. Perhaps God will create other human beings on other planets in the universe who will then be afforded an opportunity to become members of God's family as we were. Detailed specifics about the next life are few and far between in the Bible, but we are promised: "...I make all things new" (Revelation 21:5).

Q. Are we headed for a time of worldwide national catastrophes? Is this what Jesus meant in Matthew 24, when He said, 'All these are the beginning of sorrows'? Is the worst yet to come?

A. The answer is an emphatic YES.

Bible prophecy speaks of a time of worsening worldwide national conditions affecting all nations, but specifically singling out the peoples of the English-speaking world.

God, through the pen of the prophet Ezekiel, forewarned that fully two thirds of our people were to perish by warfare, catastrophic weather calamities, famines and resultant disease epidemics (read Ezekiel 5:12).

However, the prophet never reached ancient Israel with this prophecy. Those people had gone into captivity well over a hundred years before his time. Ezekiel 5:12 is for us today.

Much biblical prophecy is dual. The horrible penalties for disobedience listed in Leviticus 26 and Deuteronomy 28—as well as the first chapter of Joel—not only were inflicted upon ancient Israel, but are prophetic for the near future. These punishments are to fall on our peoples around the world today—barring a much-needed national repentance.

Q. Everyone at one time or another has heard that God gives warning before He sends punishment—that those who heed the warning will be spared the cataclysm. On the other hand, nearly all the apostles died by violent means. How are the violent deaths of so many repentant explained in light of this?

A. The scripture you are probably basing your first statement on is the following:

> 7 Surely the Lord God does nothing, Unless He reveals His secret to His servants the prophets. (Amos 3:7)

Bible prophecies are sometimes general overall warnings to a nation as a whole.

God also gives a general overall warning to Christians. He states through the apostle Paul that "all who desire to live godly in Christ Jesus will suffer persecution" (2 Timothy 3:12). The apostles themselves were practically promised martyrdom from the outset (see John 21:18-19; 16:1-2; 15:18-21). So, in this sense they were warned, but were not delivered from violence at the hand of unbelievers.

It is important to realize that there is a difference between suffering for righteousness' sake (1 Peter 1:6-7; 3:14; 4:12-16) and suffering for one's personal or national sins. God in His wisdom did allow the apostles to go through various trials and even martyrdom for the gospel's sake. This was in spite of the fact that they were repentant, righteous servants of His.

In contrast, the entire wicked city of Nineveh received a reprieve from destruction when God saw how enthusiastically they repented. Although these people were probably not leading deeply spiritual lives even after their repentance, God gave them mercy.

Reviewing the lives of all of God's servants as recorded in the Bible, it is obvious that one's spiritual state does not necessarily mean one will not have tests and trials. Since Christians often look to suffer disproportionately more than others in this age (1 Peter 4:17—understand it is for a purpose (Romans 8:28).

One of the writers of the Psalms observed that the wicked often seemed blessed while righteous suffer. But he also realized that in the end God will see to it that all these seeming injustices will be resolved (Psalm 73; cf. Ezekiel 18:25-29). It is better to suffer as a Christian (1 Peter 4:12-16) as the end it better than for non-believers (cf. 1 Peter 4:17).

The THIRD Commandment

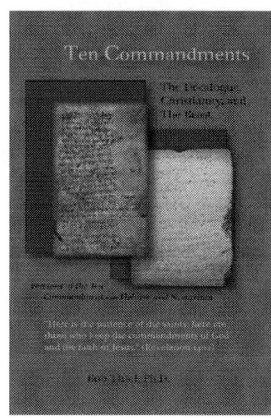

By Bob Thiel

Do words matter?

Certainly.

Jesus taught:

> 34 ... For out of the abundance of the heart the mouth speaks. 35 A good man out of the good treasure of his heart brings forth good things, and an evil man out of the evil treasure brings forth evil things. 36 But I say to you that for every idle word men may speak, they will give account of it in the day of judgment.
>
> 37 For by your words you will be justified, and by your words you will be condemned. (Matthew 12:37)

What you speak does matter, and that is more than not bearing false witness.

We see much vulgarity in the world today.

The United States has long been the world leader in producing movies. Yet, because some believe that those having a 'G' (General Audience) rating could harm their marketing efforts, vulgar and lust-provoking language is often included in movies.

Such things should not be done (cf. 1 Timothy 6:9-10).

Jesus taught:

> 20 What comes out of a man, that defiles a man. 21 For from within, out of the heart of men, proceed evil thoughts ... blasphemy, pride, foolishness" (Mark 7:20-22).

When people curse to have God condemn someone, in their pride, they act like that they have that type authority, which they do not. For:

> 10 ... those who walk according to the flesh in the lust of uncleanness and despise authority. They are presumptuous, self-willed. They are not afraid to speak evil of dignitaries (2 Peter 2:10)

Here is the third commandment from the Book of Exodus:

> 7 "You shall not take the name of the Lord your God in vain, for the Lord will not hold him guiltless who takes His name in vain. (Exodus 20:7)

We need to be careful about using God's name. And this goes beyond not cursing.

Many claim that God has done this or that for them, when He has not. Various ones claim many things are God's will, even their bad choices, when that is not the will of God.

We are not to be presumptuous:

> 13 Keep back Your servant also from presumptuous sins; (Psalms 19:13)

So be careful before you declare something is God's will.

Christians should further see what the Apostle Paul wrote:

> 8 But now you yourselves are to put off all these: anger, wrath, malice, blasphemy, filthy language out of your mouth. (Colossians 3:8)

So, we see that the New Testament prohibits both

blasphemy, which is speaking improperly about God, as well as filthy language, which can also include speaking against God.

Notice also Christians are to even control their thoughts:

> 5 casting down arguments and every high thing that exalts itself against the knowledge of God, bringing every thought into captivity to the obedience of Christ, (2 Corinthians 10:5)

Furthermore, Christians are admonished to:

> 29 Let no corrupt word proceed out of your mouth, but what is good for necessary edification, that it may impart grace to the hearers. (Ephesians 4:29)

So, more than just not taking God's name in vain and not thinking bad, Christians are to speak that which is good.

Because "holy and reverend is his {God's} name" (Psalm 111:9, KJV), we do not refer to ministers or others with titles like "reverend." And because Jesus said, "Do not call anyone on earth your father; for One is your Father, He who is in heaven" (Matthew 23:9), we do not refer to religious leaders as "father" (that title is basically reserved for our physical fathers and our Father in heaven).

Please also consider that those who are not truly Christians are taking God's name in vain if they call themselves Christians as are those who curse with God's name.

(It should be noted that blasphemy against the Holy Spirit—Matthew 12:31-32 and Hebrews 6:4-6—involves turning against the truth by the truly converted as well as the ways of God, and is not a result of inadvertently cursing.)

What About 'Sacred Names'?

Some believe that it is wrong for Christians to use terms like God, Jesus, or Lord. They believe that this is using God's name in vain.

Typically, because of what is called the 'tetragrammaton,' YHVH (translated as 'LORD' or 'Lord' in many Protestant and Catholic Bibles), these people believe that the Father must be called Jehovah, Yahveh, or Yahweh. They normally prefer some version of the term Yeshua to refer to Jesus.

While it can be proper to use terms like Yahveh or Y'eshua, many fail to realize that the New Testament was basically written in Greek. Though some claim that the New Testament was originally written in Hebrew or Aramaic, scholars have concluded that the Greek New Testament does NOT show signs of being translated (other than obviously various statements of Jesus made in Aramaic, etc.). Plus, at least one Aramaic linguist has declared that the type of Aramaic that the 'Aramaic New Testament' has been translated from did not exist in Jesus' area during his time. Therefore totally disproving the position that the New Testament was originally written in Aramaic.

The reality is that the inspired New Testament does use words properly translated into English as God, Jesus, or Lord and does not use words like Yahweh or Y'shua.

What are commonly referred to as 'sacred names' simply were not preserved in the Greek New Testament, hence they are not a Christian requirement.

Ignoring what language the New Testament was originally written in, consider that when Jesus was dying and prayed, He did NOT refer to His Father as Yahveh or Yahweh:

> 46 And about the ninth hour Jesus cried out with a loud voice, saying, "Eli, Eli, lama sabachthani?" that is, "My God, My God, why have You forsaken Me?" (Matthew 27:46)

Notice that the biblical translation was that Jesus was calling out to God. In the entire New Testament, Jesus is NEVER quoted using any of the 'sacred names' that many claim is necessary.

This clearly demonstrates that Jesus did NOT feel He had to refer to God the Father with any so-called 'sacred name.' While Christians are to be respectful, it is not biblically correct to insist on 'sacred names.'

Furthermore, since there are no vowels in ancient Hebrew nor Aramaic, no one is 100% certain as to how various names in the Old Testament were pronounced. And in the New Testament Greek, Jesus' name is not written as Y'eshua—it is closer to Ieesous.

It should also be understood that Jesus told His followers to refer to His Father as 'Father' when praying (Matthew 6:9)—not any version of YHVH.

The New Testament most certainly DOES NOT require sacred names, and not using them is NOT a violation of the third commandment.

Do Not Swear

Jesus taught:

> 33 Again you have heard that it was said to those of old, 'You shall not swear falsely, but shall perform your oaths to the Lord.' 34 But I say to you, do not swear at all: neither by heaven, for it is God's throne; 35 nor by the earth, for it is His footstool; nor by Jerusalem, for it is the city of the great King. 36 Nor shall you swear by your head, because you cannot make one hair white or black. 37 But let your 'Yes' be 'Yes,' and your 'No,' 'No.' For whatever is more than these is from the evil one. (Matthew 5:33-37)

James taught:

> 12 But above all, my brethren, do not swear, either by heaven or by earth or with any other oath. But let your "Yes" be "Yes," and your "No," "No," lest you fall into judgment. (James 5:12)

Swearing implies a certainty that one can make something come to pass. But only God can do that.

Therefore, traditionally, true Christians have not sworn oaths or done similar things.

From a legal perspective, many societies allow one to affirm that they are being truthful when providing testimony or signing documents. And providing affirmation is what we in the Continuing Church of God advise Christians to do when asked to swear.

Euphemistically Using God's Name in Vain

Satan has influenced society (Ephesians 2:2) and many people curse using God's name in vain.

Satan has deceived the whole world (Revelation 12:9). Many believe that they can say versions of these curses with semi-substitutes.

The common abuses of God's name are obvious to any true Christian, and real Christians will zealously avoid using or thinking them. But other, more subtle, vain uses of God's name can creep into our language, and we should just as diligently guard against them. These wrong words and phrases are euphemisms substituted for blatant misuses of God's name, but are also wrong.

Various ones vainly make statements like, 'Oh, my God!' when they are not praying to God. Many use statements, like, 'Oh, my gosh!' or 'good gracious' or 'good grief' or 'Oh, my goodness!' which are essentially euphemistic ways to say the same thing. In electronic communications, "OMG" is also used a lot. Such should not be done. Those may sound innocent enough at first, but think about them a moment and it's obvious that they really are slang expressions for God's name. As a parent, be sure your children are aware of the double meaning of these common words.

Many, when upset, scream, 'Jesus!,' again not in prayer. Others, do the same basic thing when they cry out, 'Geez' or 'Gee whiz!' Terms like crud (when used as a substitute for the word Christ), egad, and golly also fall into this category.

There are also other improper statements.

Now, we are not trying to teach that making unintended misstatements is something we should judge others on—but as Christians it is something that we should strive not to do.

Do not euphemistically use God's name in vain.

Do not call yourself Christian if you will not be willing to live as Jesus wanted you to (cf. 1 Corinthians 11:1; 1 John 2:6).

Perhaps it should be mentioned that the reason we in the Continuing Church of God do not say, 'God bless you' after someone sneezes is because that tradition is based on the unbiblical notion that an evil spirit may enter someone who sneezes and must be warded off with some type of a spell.

If someone is truly ill they can pray and others can also pray for them (James 5:13-14).

Third Commandment Before Sinai, from Jesus, and After Jesus' Death

The Bible shows the third commandment was in place before Mt. Sinai:

> "nor shall you profane the name of your God... for all these abominations the men of the land have done, who were before you, and thus the land is defiled" (Leviticus 18:21,27). "It may be that my sons have sinned and cursed God in their hearts" (Job 1:5). "Curse God and die!" (Job 2:9). Interestingly, those called of God are not to be cursed either, "And I will curse him who curses you" (Genesis 12:3).

Jesus taught and expanded the third commandment:

> "pray: Our Father in heaven, Hallowed be Your name" (Matthew 6:9). "Therefore I say to you, every sin and blasphemy will be forgiven men, but the blasphemy against the Spirit will not be forgiven men" (Matthew 12:31). "For out of the heart proceed evil thoughts, ...blasphemies. These are the things which defile a man" (Matthew 15:19-20). "What comes out of a man, that defiles a man. 21 For from within, out of the heart of men, proceed evil thoughts ... blasphemy, pride, foolishness" (Mark 7:20-22).

After Jesus was resurrected, the New Testament taught the third commandment:

> "they are all under sin...Whose mouth is full of cursing and bitterness" (Romans 3:9,14). "Let all ... evil speaking be put away from you" (Ephesians 4:31). "But now you yourselves are to put off all these: ... blasphemy, filthy language out of your mouth" (Colossians 3:8). "they may learn not to blaspheme" (1 Timothy 1:20). But know this, that in the last days perilous times will come: For men will be ... blasphemers" (2 Timothy 3:1,2). "Out of the same mouth proceed blessing and cursing. My brethren, these things ought not to be so" (James 3:10). "He is the antichrist who denies the Father and the Son" (1 John 2:22).

Do not take God's name in vain.

FREE *Continuing Church of God* Books and Booklets
at www.ccog.org/books

Christians: AMBASSADORS

Continuing History of the Church of God

Dating: A Key to Success in Marriage

Faith for Those God has Called and Chosen

STUDY THE BIBLE COURSE

Lesson 15: What is "Hell"?

Published 2019 by the *Continuing* Church of God

> Preface: This course is highly based upon the personal correspondence course developed in 1954 that began under the direction of the late C. Paul Meredith in the old Radio Church of God. Various portions have been updated for the 21st century (though much of the original writing has been retained). It also has more scriptural references, as well as information and questions not in the original course. Unless otherwise noted, scriptural references are to the NKJV, copyright Thomas Nelson Publishing, used by permission. The KJV, sometimes referred to as the Authorized Version is also often used. Additionally, Catholic-approved translations such as the New Jerusalem Bible (NJB) are sometimes used as are other translations.

You are probably familiar this world's idea of a horrifying, nightmarish place of never-ending torture for lost sinners.

But is that what the Bible teaches?

It's time we QUIT 'swallowing' the IDEAS and THEORIES of confused humanity, and begin STUDYING the truth for ourselves in GOD'S Word!

Now, we in the *Continuing* Church of God rarely use the word 'hell' as its often understood meaning in modern times is in error. The word 'hell' originally meant to cover or to hide. Another old meaning of the word was 'a tailor's receptacle' according to *Merriam-Webster*. Over a century ago, it tended to mean being underground.

There are three different words in the New Testament--Hades, Gehenna, or Tartaroosas--which the King James Version of the Bible translated as 'hell' And not one of them means what most people think the word hell means.

The fact of the three different Greek words being translated as hell, as well as various understandings and traditions, has resulted in confusion concerning what the Bible is teaching related to punishment. Furthermore, since the term has become highly used in cursing and in various vulgarities it is often not appropriate to use.

The Common Idea

Before going further, let's notice a generally accepted common belief in the Western world about hell. Here's the terse and brief summation of this popular belief, from the *Encyclopedia Britannica:*

> Hell, in many religious traditions, the abode, usually beneath the earth, of the unredeemed dead or the spirits of the damned. In its archaic sense, the term hell refers to the underworld, a deep pit or distant land of shadows where the dead are gathered. From the underworld come dreams, ghosts, and demons, and in its most terrible precincts sinners pay—some say eternally—the penalty for their crimes. The underworld is often imagined as a place of punishment rather than merely of darkness and decomposition because of the widespread belief that a moral universe requires judgment and retribution—crime must not pay. More broadly, hell figures in religious cosmologies as the opposite of heaven, the nadir of the cosmos, and the land where God is not. In world literature the journey to hell is a perennial motif of hero legends and quest stories, and hell itself is the preeminent symbol of evil, alienation, and despair.

Many believe some version of the above.

April - June 2019

From the Pagans

Now where, and how, did this popular belief about hell ORIGINATE?

The *Encyclopedia Americana* states:

> The main features of hell as conceived by Hindu, Persian, Egyptian, Grecian, and Christian theologians ARE ESSENTIALLY THE SAME.

The Western religious leaders through the Middle Ages borrowed the doctrine of eternal torture FROM THE PAGAN PHILOSOPHERS. Certain of these writers of the Middle Ages had such tremendous influence on the Christian-professing world, that their writings and teachings came to be generally accepted and believed, until it became the doctrine of the Christian-professing world.

Among these influential writers were Augustine (345-430 A.D.), and Dante Alighieri (1265-1321 A.D.). Dante wrote a popular book now known as, "The Divine Comedy," in three parts – *Inferno, Purgatorio,* and *Paradiso.*

There is another book titled "Dante and His Influence," which sums up the history of the Christian-professing doctrine of hell. This factual history says that:

> ... of all poets of modern times, Dante Alighieri was, perhaps, the greatest educator. He possibly had a greater influence on the course of civilization than any other man since his day...
>
> Dante ... wrote, in incomprehensible verse, an imaginative and lurid account of a dismal hell—a long poem containing certain phrases which caught the attention of the world, such as "ALL HOPE ABANDON, YE, WHO ENTER HERE!" ... to the Inferno ... (Page TN. Dante and His Influence. Charles Scribner's Sons, 1922, pp. 3,7,8).

His *'Inferno'* poem was based on the writings by the ancient pagan writers Virgil and Plato.

Dante's writing had a tremendous impression and influence on popular Catholic thought and teaching, as well as, later, many Protestants. Dante is reported to have been so fascinated and enraptured by the ideas and philosophies of PLATO and VIRGIL, who were pagan philosophers, that he reportedly believed they were divinely inspired. Dante has 'Virgil' accompanying him to see various levels of the inferno, purgatario, and paradiso.

In 1320, Dante's set of poems was original titled "The Comedy." Yet beginning in 1555 it became known as "The Divine Comedy." Many improperly took Dante's descriptions as at least indicative of, if not actually, God's plan for humanity.

As far as "purgatorio," now more commonly called purgatory, goes, the Roman Catholics tend to consider that it is like the inferno and is also a place of torment. Their 15/16th century saint Catherine of Genoa claimed that those in purgatory, "suffer torments which no tongue can describe nor any intelligence comprehend."

Yet, the Roman Catholic purgatory is not in the Bible. Nor was it part of the original Christian faith. Purgatory was essentially adopted by Rome in the 6th century with other clarifications (such as related to 'indulgences') added later.

Much of the world's concept of 'hell' and purgatory is a product of centuries of human thinking on the great problem of reward and punishment associated with human deeds. It did NOT COME AS A REVELATION FROM GOD, but is rather the product of HUMAN REASON to decide what ONLY GOD CAN REVEAL!

What About the Billions and Billions of Heathen?

Let us consider where this concept of hell, if true, leads us.

On this earth there are close to eight billion people, and some believe that there have been over one hundred billion!

Throughout history, people living in some of the most populous lands as well as remote places on the earth have NEVER SO MUCH AS HEARD 'THE ONLY NAME BY WHICH HUMANS MAY BE SAVED' – the name of

JESUS CHRIST, For your Bible says, "... there is no other name under heaven given among men by which we must be saved"(Acts 4:12).

Now consider the fact that even most who heard the name have been properly told about salvation—they have not known the truth about Christian salvation. So this means that multiple BILLIONS of people on this earth have lived, and DIED, without having SAVING KNOWLEDGE! Now think what that means.

If all UNsaved have gone immediately to a burning hell at death – as commonly believed – then most of the people who have ever lived on this earth have been consigned there without ever having been given so much as a CHANCE to escape it! They, according to the teachings of some churches, are ETERNALLY LOST IN TORMENTING 'HELL FIRE!'

Can you really believe THAT IS the plan by which an all-wise, all-merciful, LOVING GOD IS working out His purpose here below?

WHAT IS THE TRUTH?

We face these alternatives: Either the Holy Bible is the INSPIRED Word of God, by which the Creator REVEALS the TRUTH on this subject, or else we must fling up our hands and confess we JUST DON'T KNOW – we are IGNORANT on the question. We must believe what the Bible says, or we can believe NOTHING, if we are rational and honest!

IS there even such a thing as 'hell fire'? What does the BIBLE say about it?

Didn't Jesus say something about 'hell fire'?

Yes, but not as commonly understood.

We are about ready for the actual lesson. But first, read these instructions.

Before You Begin

Is your Bible in front of you? If not, go GET YOUR BIBLE – or Bibles if you have more than one translation.

Also have several sheets of paper, and a pen, pencil or computer so that you can MAKE NOTES to help you in remembering what you learn.

Remember – you must open your Bible to EVERY PASSAGE. Try not to say to yourself, "Oh, I think I know what the scripture is referring to" – and then pass over it. You need to KEEP YOUR NOSE IN THE BIBLE, SO to speak. You should READ and REREAD and STUDY EVERY PASSAGE in your Bible. Don't forget, this is a BIBLE STUDY COURSE – not just a study of these lessons we send you. This lesson is intended to DIRECT YOU to the Bible – to help you LEARN the TRUTH of God's Word.

Now with your Bible, a good dictionary, and concordance, if you have one, and your stationery all in front of you, here is the METHOD of study. Write down neatly on your paper the lesson TITLE. Next write down the lesson number. As you come to each question section, write down ITS HEADING. Then, at the lefthand margin, print the NUMBER OF EACH QUESTION as you come to it, and WRITE DOWN THE BIBLE ANSWERS, together with any PERTINENT IDEAS that may come to your mind.

Be sure to WRITE OUT THE SCRIPTURE which answers each question. Writing the answers and any comments you wish to make as you go along WILL HELP YOU GREATLY IN REVIEWING AND REMEMBERING WHAT YOU LEARN.

Now we are ready to begin this lesson.

LESSON 15

Christ Spoke of 'Gehenna Fire'

1. What PUNISHMENT did Christ warn would happen to those who would not QUIT SINNING? Mark 9:43. Did He say they would "go into hell" (KJV)? And did He say there would be a FIRE there? Same verse.

Then there really is a hell, since CHRIST says so, isn't there?

COMMENT: Well, 'hell' is an English word. When Mark recorded these words Christ had spoken, he wrote them in the GREEK language. The Greek word which Mark was inspired to write down, which was translated 'hell' in the KJV, was 'Gehenna'.

And since this same verse also says the sinner is 'to go into hell, INTO THE FIRE' (KJV), it follows that Christ clearly stated here that the incorrigible will receive punishment by FIRE as their ultimate fate.

Note that Christ associated the Greek word Gehenna with FIRE.

2. Did Christ, FOR GREATER EMPHASIS, repeat, in Mark 9:45, that this punishment by fire would befall those who CONTINUE to sin?

COMMENT: Mark wrote down the SAME Greek word 'Gehenna' here in verse 45 that he used in verse 43. Those who translated this Greek word into English, when they made the English Bible, often have selected the English word 'hell' to represent this Greek word 'Gehenna'.

3. Did Christ repeat a third time, for the greatest emphasis, that anyone who PERSISTENTLY SERVES SIN will receive this punishment by Gehenna 'FIRE' – 'HELL fire'? Verse 47.

COMMENT: Again, the Greek word which Mark used in this verse was GEHENNA.

GEHENNA is certainly tied in with fire.

Generally, in CCOG sermons, we would use the term Gehenna (as certain English translations correctly do) when that is the actual Greek word used to better help people understand what Jesus was actually teaching.

English Word "Hell" Misapplied

Keep in mind, as we read his material, that the Old Testament was originally written in the Hebrew language, and that the New Testament was originally written in the Greek language.

On the use of the word 'hell' in the New and Old Testament, let's read what an old Bible dictionary, edited by James Hastings, a leading authority on such technical matters, says:

> In our Authorized Version the word 'hell' is unfortunately used as the rendering OF THREE DISTINCT WORDS, WITH DIFFERENT MEANINGS. It represents, 1. the 'sheol' of the Hebrew Old Testament, and the 'hades' in the New Testament ... It is now AN ENTIRELY MISLEADING RENDERING, especially in the New Testament passages. The English revisers, therefore, have substituted 'Hades' [going back to the original Greek word] for 'hell' in the New Testament .... In the American revision the word 'hell' is entirely discarded in this connexion ....
>
> The word 'hell' is used 2. as equivalent to [the Greek word] 'tartaros' (II Peter 2:4), ... and, 3. more properly as the equivalent of [the Greek word] 'gehenna' (Hastings J., ed. Dictionary of the Bible, Vol. 2. 1900, pp. 343-344)

So, we see that the real MEANINGS of three different Greek words – 'hade', ('sheol' in Old Testament), 'tartaros', and 'gehenna' – have been confused with each other because translators have attempted to make the ONE English word 'hell' cover all THREE meanings! But now let us amplify the foregoing facts.

The original Old Testament HEBREW word 'sheol' and the New Testament Greek word 'hades' mean basically the same thing. These original words have been translated 'grave' in many places in the Bible.

> THE WORD 'SHEOL',... It is never used by Moses or the Prophets in the sense of a place of torment after death; and in no way conflicts with the statement already proved, that the Law of Moses deals wholly in temporal rewards and punishments.
>
> This position, also, I wish to fortify by the testimony of Orthodox critics, men of learning and candor. They know, and therefore they speak.
>
> 1. CHAPMAN. "Sheol, in itself considered, has

no connection with future punishment." Cited by Balfour, First Inquiry.

2. DR. ALLEN, quoted above, says: "The term sheol does not seem to mean, with certainty, anything more than the state of the dead in their deep abode."

3. DR. CAMPBELL. "Sheol signifies the state of the dead without regard to their happiness or misery."

4. DR. WHITBY. "Sheol throughout the Old Testament signifies not the place of punishment, or of the souls of bad men only, but the grave only, or the place of death." (Thayer TB. THE ORIGIN AND HISTORY OF THE Doctrine of Endless Punishment. 1855; Universal Publishing House 1871)

Sheol is a reference to the grave, as is the word hades.

'Hell' is an old English word, and over 400 years ago, when the 'Authorized Version' (also known as the King James Version) was translated, the people of England commonly talked of "putting their potatoes in HELL for the winter" – a good way of preserving potatoes – for the word mainly then meant A HOLE IN THE GROUND which was covered up – a dark and silent place – like a GRAVE.

But PAGAN TEACHINGS gaining popular acceptance caused people to apply to the English word 'hell' the FALSE MEANING which came out of the lurid IMAGINATIONS of Dante and some others.

Note, too, that the Greek word TARTAROS, which has also been translated into the English word "hell," occurs only once in the New Testament (2 Peter 2:4) and does not refer to humans, but to the RESTRAINED condition of fallen angels. Its meaning, translated into English, is 'darkness of the material universe', or 'dark abyss', or 'prison'.

Now, what about Gehenna? This Greek word represents 'the Valley of HINNOM which lay just outside of Jerusalem and was the place refuse was constantly being burned up'. It is first referred to in scripture in Joshua 15:8. It was also associated with pagan fire practices in 2 Kings 23:10; 2 Chronicles 28:3, 33:6; Jeremiah 7:31-32, 19:2-6, & 32:35.

Trash, filth, and the dead bodies of animals and DESPISED CRIMINALS were thrown into Gehenna. Ordinarily, everything thrown into this valley was DESTROYED by fire. Christ used it to picture the terrible fate of UNREPENTANT SINNERS!

But of the foregoing, remember this especially: In MOST of the passages of the NEW TESTAMENT where we see the word 'hell' in our English Bible translations, the ORIGINAL GREEK WORD was a DIFFERENT word than the word Gehenna. This other different word is the word 'hades' – which does NOT refer to FIRE at all, but has an entirely different meaning.

Yet many translators have used the ONE English word – 'HELL' – for these TWO entirely different GREEK words that have TWO ENTIRELY DIFFERENT MEANINGS!

Let's understand.

1. Does Luke 12:5 contain the word 'hell'?

COMMENT: Many English translations show that. However, were you to look up the ORIGINAL GREEK WORD that is here translated into the English word 'hell', you would find it to be GEHENNA.

Theologically, GEHENNA ESSENTIALLY MEANS A PLACE OF DESTRUCTIVE PUNISHMENT, and Christ indicated this would be carried out by FIRE!

2. BUT now notice the SAME ENGLISH WORD 'HELL' in Acts 2:31, KJV!

COMMENT: To read the ENGLISH translation of these two scriptures – Luke 12:5 and Acts 2:31 – it would SEEM that the word 'hell' has the same meaning in both. BUT the original GREEK word which is translated by the English word 'hell' in Acts 2:31 in the KJV is HADES.

'Hades' means 'GRAVE'!

HADES is put for the grave, or the state of the

dead. Our translators have so rendered it in 1 Cor. 15:55. "O death, where is thy sting? O grave (hades), where is thy victory?" ...

DR. FAIRBAIRN, the learned professor of divinity in the College of Glasgow, and whose volumes on 'Prophecy' and 'Typology' have given him high rank among biblical students and interpreters, says without reserve, "Beyond doubt, sheol, like hades, was regarded as the abode after death, alike of the good and the bad." (Thayer)

Sheol, hades, tartaroos, and Gehenna have often been mistranslated as the same word (though sheol and hades do basically mean the same).

We can plainly see that the English word 'hell' has been translated from words with DIFFERENT meanings! So when if come to the word 'hell' in our New Testament, we must carefully distinguish whether it is speaking of punishment by fire, or of the grave where the dead lie quietly buried. THESE ARE TWO VASTLY DIFFERENT MEANINGS FOR WHAT MANY THINK IS THE SAME WORD.

When you see the word 'hell' in your Bible, if you do not know what term it is translated from, you may wish to look it up in an EXHAUSTIVE CONCORDANCE or some type of Greek scriptural text, if you want to BETTER know its true meaning.

Where To After Death?

When an incorrigible sinner dies, what happens? When such a sinner is interred into the grave, does he/she lie quietly and silently there, knowing NOTHING and awaiting the RESURRECTION? Or, at death, does the "soul" of the sinner descend immediately into an inferno of eternal 'hell fire' torture for sins?

What is the truth? What does GOD reveal about the state of man after death?

1. Do men and beasts all go to ONE place – the SAME place – when they die? Ecclesiastes 3:19-20. Consider that you probably have never seriously heard of beasts going to "hell" to be TORTURED, have you?

2. Does this same event – returning to ONE PLACE – happen to both the righteous and the wicked? Ecclesiastes 9:2. Then one doesn't go to heaven at death, and the other to hell, do they?

3. Where then do all go after death – back to the DUST from which they were made? Genesis 3:19. Does Ecclesiastes 3:20 verify this?

4. Does Psalm 146:4 show that no one is able to think after perishing? Are the dead unable to remember God? Psalm 6:5. Then ALL mental and physical processes of an individual come to a HALT at death, don't they? How much do the dead know? Ecclesiastes 9:5. Then isn't it true that a dead person has no more consciousness than a dead animal has?

5. What PLACE does God say someone goes at death? Ecclesiastes 9:10. Did Job realize he would go to the GRAVE after death? Job 17:13, KJV. Were worms of the EARTH to be his companions? Verse 14, KJV. The Hebrew term in Ecclesiastes 9:10 and Job 17:13 is sheol.

6. Must ALL people die at least once? Hebrews 9:27. Does 1 Corinthians 15:22 verify this? Did Christ take upon Himself the same mortal flesh of which we are composed? Hebrews 2:14. And didn't He also have to go to the GRAVE as all mortals do? Acts 2:31, KJV.

COMMENT: The original Greek word which has been translated 'hell' in this verse is 'hades' (as the NKJV renders it) which, as you now know, means the 'GRAVE'. Christ did NOT go down into a fiery hell, but merely into a GRAVE. God does not sentence anyone to a fiery hell immediately after they die, but merely to the GRAVE.

7. Was Jacob, in speaking of his son whom he thought to be dead, certain he was already in a GRAVE? Genesis 37:35.

COMMENT: How overpowering the evidence is that the unrepentant sinner, or anyone else, does not go to a place of torment at death! They go to the GRAVE--SHEOL, where they know ABSOLUTELY NOTHING!

Resurrected to Judgment

You may have heard preaching about people going directly to the fiery tortures of 'hell' when they die. But have you ever heard of a JUDGMENT – a FORMAL SENTENCING – of these people by God, BEFORE they go to their punishment?

What did Jesus mean when He said in John 5:28-29, RSV: "the hour is coming, when all who are in the tombs will hear His voice and come forth ... those who have done evil, to the resurrection of JUDGMENT"? (Note: Unlike what the NKJV shows 'condemnation', the Greek word kriseoos should be properly translated as judgment, which the NJB, AFV, BSB, NASB, ASV, DRB, RVS, DBT, ESV, WNY, and YLT show.)

Christ said the judgment of the evil dead who are now in their graves, is yet ahead. Then how could they now be receiving punishment when they have not, as yet, even received JUDGMENT for their sins? The two ideas obviously contradict each other!

When and where DO the dead go from their graves? Here's what YOUR Bible reveals.

1. Is there to be a day of judgment? 2 Peter 2:9; Revelation 20:11-13.

2. Is there to be a time when the unjust are judged for PUNISHMENT? 2 Peter 2:9.

3. When is this judgment to be? Hebrews 9:27; Revelation 20:5a.

COMMENT: It is plain that people will receive final judgment from God at some time AFTER they die.

4. Is God able to bring people up alive from the GRAVE? 1 Samuel 2:6. Does Revelation 20:11-13 prove there is to be a great FUTURE "resurrection to judgment"?

COMMENT: ALL the dead on land or in the sea, wherever they may be, incorrigible and otherwise, are to be RESURRECTED TO 'JUDGMENT' IN THE FUTURE (Revelation 20:11-13). No one is, or ever has been, down in a fiery 'hell' dancing around on hot coals, shrieking in terror and torment!

'The Wages of Sin Is DEATH'

What is the PENALTY – the 'WAGES', or reward – of sin? Is it ETERNAL CONSCIOUSNESS in torment, or is it ETERNAL OBLIVION? Let's study further and see.

1. What does Paul warn will be the judgment of those who, knowing God's commands, WILFULLY SIN against them? Hebrews 10:26-27. Notice that this judgment comes on people because they SIN WILFULLY.

2. And what is the 'wages of sin'? Romans 6:23.

COMMENT: The 'wages of sin is DEATH!' — ETERNAL DEATH for every part of you! 'Death' is the OPPOSITE of 'life'!

3. Does Jesus compare the false ministers to trees that don't bring forth 'good fruit' – GOOD WORKS? Matthew 7:15-19. What did He say would happen to such people? Verse 19. Isn't wood put into a fire to be BURNED UP? Did Christ say ALL people who do not bring forth good fruit will be CAST INTO FIRE? Matthew 7:17-19, 23.

4. What did Christ warn would happen to those who do not repent of their sinful ways? Luke 13:3. Does 'perish' mean to CEASE existing, or CONTINUE living? Look up the meaning in a dictionary.

'Gehenna Fire' Will DESTROY!

God has NOT decreed eternal LIFE in torment for the incorrigible sinner! The punishment revealed in the Bible is eternal DEATH – cessation of life forever. Eternal LIFE IS something we do not now have – it is a GIFT of God given at the resurrection to those that OBEY Him. Eternal life and eternal death are contrasted all through your Bible!

Now notice what God says He WILL do with the sinners – the incorrigibly wicked on whom He has decreed, 'the wages of sin is DEATH' (Romans 6:23).

1. Did Christ show by His parable of the tares that there was to be a future harvest? Matthew 13:30.

COMMENT: In this parable Christ likened the earth

to a 'field' (verse 24), the obedient people to 'wheat' (verses 25, 29), and the disobedient to 'tares' (verses 25, 29, 30).

2. Did Christ say the EVIL PEOPLE – the 'tares' – will be BURNED? Matthew 13:30.

3. Does Psalm 37:20, KJV also indicate the that ultimate fate of the wicked will be destruction by FIRE?

4. Is there coming a time that will be extremely hot? Malachi 4:1. Will this time be so hot that it will BURN UP THE WICKED? Same verse. Since this heat consumes the wicked, will only the righteous be left?

5. Will the righteous ultimately walk on the wicked? Malachi 4:3. In what FORM will the wicked be? Same verse. Who will burn the wicked up?

6. What did Christ warn the false preachers of His day – the Scribes and Pharisees – would be their fate? Matthew 23:33.

COMMENT: The original Greek word translated here as 'hell', is Gehenna – meaning the Valley of Hinnom. Christ was referring to the fire that burned in the Valley of Hinnom as a type of complete destruction of the wicked by fire. Christ was thus asking these sinning ministers how THEY could possibly escape a DESTRUCTION BY FIRE such as they saw daily at the city dump, located in the VALLEY OF HINNOM just outside of Jerusalem.

Look at the Berean Literal Translation:

> 33 Serpents! Offspring of vipers! How shall you escape from the sentence of Gehenna? (Matthew 23:33, BLB)

Notice the end result:

> 1 "For behold, the day is coming, Burning like an oven, And all the proud, yes, all who do wickedly will be stubble. And the day which is coming shall burn them up,"Says the Lord of hosts, "That will leave them neither root nor branch..." (Malachi 4:1, NKJV)

The biblical fire WILL CONSUME THE DISOBEDIENT! NEVER will they exist again. This is a fearful warning to those who know God's truth and still REFUSE to obey it!

"For the wages of sin is DEATH, but the GIFT of God is eternal life in Christ Jesus our Lord." (Romans 6:23) If you believe this scripture means what it says, then you know the TRUTH. But, unfortunately, most theologians AND THEIR BLIND FOLLOWERS try to TWIST and DISTORT what Paul said into something else – to eternal life in torment.

The wages, or reward, of sin is shown to be DEATH, but ETERNAL LIFE IS stated to be a GIFT from God – NOT SOMETHING WE ALREADY HAVE.

DEATH means just that – cessation of life and consciousness – TOTAL OBLIVION! In spite of the vain attempts of many preachers to make DEATH mean SEPARATION FROM GOD, YOU CANNOT reconcile this with Scripture. Nor does DEATH mean ETERNAL LIFE in the horrifying torments in Gehenna.

The false doctrine of a non-consuming, but only torturing of an imaginary 'hell fire', which has been used to frighten so many deceived human beings, is a preposterous LIE! Its author is the father of lies – Satan the Devil! (John 8:44.) If you are one who has been deceived by this doctrine, and are suffering mental torment because of it, MAY GOD HELP YOU TO UNDERSTAND THE TRUTH!

The Destruction of Earth's Surface by Fire

And now comes a most interesting revelation! Of what does Gehenna itself consist? Read now IN YOUR OWN BIBLE what God the Father reveals Gehenna fire is GOING TO BE.

If people persist in disobeying God, WHERE did Christ warn they would ultimately find themselves? Mark 9:43-45. Won't they find themselves in GEHENNA FIRE – A PLACE OF DESTRUCTION?

1. Are the sexually immoral, murderers, liars, and such types – people who use the various

members of their bodies, such as their hands, feet and eyes to DISOBEY the commands of God – ultimately to find themselves in this 'lake' of fire and brimstone? Revelation 21:8.

COMMENT: A LARGE FIRE often has the APPEARANCE of a fiery lake. That is WHY this colossal world-end FIRE IS COMPARED to a 'LAKE' of fire! It is not a usual water-filled lake.

2. Will it cause their death? Revelation 21:8. WHICH death will it cause? Same verse.

COMMENT: ALL of us must die ONCE, because we just 'wear out' (Hebrews 9:27), but if anyone dies the SECOND death, referred to in Revelation 21:8, it is because that person has been JUDGED guilty of persistent disobedience. The SECOND death is ETERNAL death!

3. Does Revelation 20:13-14 verify the fact that the evil will be cast into this coming lake of fire only AFTER the coming final judgment?

4. Will ALL mortals NOT ultimately written in the book of (eternal) life be cast into this lake of fire? Revelation 20:15.

COMMENT: HERE IS God's – not some human's – but GOD'S description of what the coming fire WILL BE! It is yet in the future, having never occurred before. And nothing is said anywhere in the entire Bible about DESCENDING BENEATH the earth into this final Gehenna fire or of TORTURE for all eternity! Rather, the Bible shows DESTRUCTION for all eternity of all unsaved human beings who shall be cast into this lake of fire. Many contrary ideas have been handed down to us from paganism.

5. What is this final 'lake of fire' ACTUALLY to be – our earth's surface burning up? 2 Peter 3:10. Are basically all the things man has created on this earth to be BURNED UP along with those who will not have been born as spirit beings into the Kingdom of God? Same verse.

COMMENT: Many wonder about 2 Peter 3:10. Didn't Peter say this globe would be destroyed? Was Peter really talking about the total destruction of the earth?

Notice what the context tells us:

> 7 But the heavens and the earth which are now preserved by the same word, are reserved for fire until the day of judgment and perdition of ungodly men. (2 Peter 3:7).

This fire represents the final judgment of ungodly men. Since this is called the fire reserved until the day of judgment for the ungodly, we know this is the lake of fire which is the second death (Revelation 20:14).

An unquenchable fire is one that cannot be put out. It burns until it has consumed all combustible material. Then it dies out for lack of anything else to consume. Everything will be burned up except for spirit beings who are not affected by physical fires.

Peter used the example of Noah's Flood as a type of the future cleansing of the earth by fire, 'by which the world that then existed perished, being flooded with water' (2 Peter 3:6). Just as the earth continued to exist after the Flood, so it will continue to exist after the coming world-wide Gehenna fire.

The earth will still exist (Ecclesiastes 1:4). The simple explanation of 2 Peter 3:10 is that the surface of the earth and everything on it, including the incorrigibly wicked, will be destroyed by fire. God will then remake the surface of the earth for a habitation for Himself and the rest of the God Kingdom (Revelation 21, 22).

6. Is the lake of fire, into which the Beast and False Prophet are cast alive at Christ's second coming, a TYPE of this great worldwide fire? Revelation 19:20. What is it burning with? Same verse.

COMMENT: The small PROTOTYPE 'lake of fire' of Revelation 19:20, which will burn in the Valley of Hinnom at Christ's return, foreshadows THE final lake of fire which will consume the entire earth's surface MUCH LATER, making it a molten mass!

But this lake of fire burns with brimstone—another word for sulphur. Sulphur, depending on whether it is in dust or liquid form, burns at 375-502 degrees Fahrenheit (190-261 Celsius).

Cremation of human remains is done at temperatures

from 1400-1800 degrees Fahrenheit (760-982 Celsius).

So, while this lake of fire kills the Beast and False Prophet, it looks would leave some parts of their corpses.

Notice that people will be able to see the corpses of these two men during the millennium:

> 23 "And it shall come to pass That from one New Moon to another, And from one Sabbath to another, All flesh shall come to worship before Me," says the Lord. 24 "And they shall go forth and look Upon the corpses of the men Who have transgressed against Me. For their worm does not die, And their fire is not quenched. They shall be an abhorrence to all flesh." (Isaiah 66:23-24)

This seeing the corpses happens during the time that there are fleshly humans. This is a reference to the millennium (and possibly into the time of the Great White Throne Judgment). Since flesh will be able to see the corpses, this lake of fire is not below the surface of the earth nor out in the heavens nor on/under some other planet.

The reference to their worm (maggot) not dying also ties in with Jesus' references to Gehenna (Mark 9:43-48), which will also be discussed later in this lesson. Maggots would be expected to end up in their corpses until all that maggots can eat would be gone. Jesus' comment about their 'worm' is probably also an allegorical reference to their corruption.

What will happen to the Beast and the False Prophet will serve as a stern witness to all the rest of the world.

7. Does the Old Testament show that the Beast, the leader, the end time King of the North and King of Babylon, gets maggots or worms? Isaiah 14:3-4, 11.

Let's also see that those verses show this will be noticed during the millennium ("the day the Lord gives you rest from your sorrow"):

> 3 It shall come to pass in the day the Lord gives you rest from your sorrow, and from your fear and the hard bondage in which you were made to serve, 4 that you will take up this proverb against the king of Babylon, and say: (Isaiah 14:3-4)

> 11 Your pomp is brought down to Sheol, And the sound of your stringed instruments; The maggot is spread under you, And worms cover you. (Isaiah 14:11)

Since the millennium starts after the Beast and False Prophet were tossed into the lake of fire (cf. Revelation 19:20, 20:1-6), we know this is after the start of the millennium. We also know that was a not a world encompassing destructive fire, as the world becomes a better place during the millennium (cf. Isaiah 35:1-7).

Hence, this particular Gehenna fire must be on the earth in only a small area.

This Gehenna fire is literally (Young's Literal Translation) called an 'AGE-DURING' fire in Matthew 25:41. Although Gehenna fire will later ultimately cover the entire surface of the earth and heavens (2 Peter 3:10), its length can, literally, LAST no longer than just before New Jerusalem comes down from heaven (Revelation 22:1-4).

8. Does the Devil end up in this same Gehenna fire? Revelation 20:10

Note that the word 'are' is in italics in the KJV/NKJV related to the beast and false prophet—that use of italics is showing that the translators added a word that was not there.

Here is a more biblically accurate rendering of what that verse is showing us:

> and the Devil, who had been leading them astray, was thrown into the Lake of fire and sulphur where the Wild Beast and the false Prophet were, and day and night they will suffer torture until the Ages of the Ages. (Revelation 20:10, Weymouth New Testament)

Now the above fire is, at this point, basically localized

in the Valley of Hinnom as that is where the Beast and False prophet were tossed. It also is a lake of fire with sulphur.

This also looks to be the location that people will see Satan and/or his ashes as is prophesied:

> 12 "How you are fallen from heaven, O Lucifer, son of the morning! How you are cut down to the ground, You who weakened the nations! 13 For you have said in your heart:' I will ascend into heaven, I will exalt my throne above the stars of God; I will also sit on the mount of the congregation On the farthest sides of the north; 14 I will ascend above the heights of the clouds, I will be like the Most High.' 15 Yet you shall be brought down to Sheol, To the lowest depths of the Pit.

> 16 "Those who see you will gaze at you, And consider you, saying: 'Is this the man who made the earth tremble, Who shook kingdoms, 17 Who made the world as a wilderness And destroyed its cities, Who did not open the house of his prisoners.' (Isaiah 14:12-17)

> 13 You were in Eden, the garden of God; Every precious stone was your covering: The sardius, topaz, and diamond, Beryl, onyx, and jasper, Sapphire, turquoise, and emerald with gold. The workmanship of your timbrels and pipes Was prepared for you on the day you were created.

> 14 "You were the anointed cherub who covers; I established you; You were on the holy mountain of God; You walked back and forth in the midst of fiery stones. 15 You were perfect in your ways from the day you were created, Till iniquity was found in you.

> 16 "By the abundance of your trading You became filled with violence within, And you sinned; Therefore I cast you as a profane thing Out of the mountain of God; And I destroyed you, O covering cherub, From the midst of the fiery stones.

> 17 "Your heart was lifted up because of your beauty; You corrupted your wisdom for the sake of your splendor; I cast you to the ground, I laid you before kings, That they might gaze at you.

> 18 "You defiled your sanctuaries By the multitude of your iniquities, By the iniquity of your trading; Therefore I brought fire from your midst; It devoured you, And I turned you to ashes upon the earth In the sight of all who saw you. 19 All who knew you among the peoples are astonished at you; You have become a horror, And shall be no more forever."" (Ezekiel 28:13-19)

The New Testament says that Satan is the 'god of this age' (2 Corinthian 4:4), who has deceived the whole world and is to be permanently cast down from heaven (Revelation 12:7-9). Satan was the one in Eden and both the Old and New Testaments show he will be punished with fire.

Various ones have misunderstood verses 14- 16 of Ezekiel 28. Notice that God is speaking of the beginning of the creation in this account of Satan's original rebellion. But, just as the Bible so often uses DUAL meanings, so THIS is history and prophecy at the same time!

9. What will happen to unrepentant sinners? Revelation 20:14.

COMMENT: It will be mortal unrepentant sinners who refuse to obey God who will be tossed in the lake of fire. Their end is both sad and merciful. The second death is actually a type of mercy killing. Those who die in the lake of fire, because of the twisted thinking that led them to become worthy of such a fate in the first place, would, if given eternal life, live out immortality in misery. God puts them out of their misery while He also stops them from inflicting misery on others.

10. Is there a fire attribute to God? Deuteronomy 4:24, Hebrews 12:29.

COMMENT: A consuming fire burns things up.
Let's look at 2 Peter 3:10-12, with a Protestant and a Roman Catholic translation:

> 10 But the day of the Lord will come as a thief in the night, in which the heavens will pass away

with a great noise, and the elements will melt with fervent heat; both the earth and the works that are in it will be burned up. 11 Therefore, since all these things will be dissolved, what manner of persons ought you to be in holy conduct and godliness, 12 looking for and hastening the coming of the day of God, because of which the heavens will be dissolved, being on fire, and the elements will melt with fervent heat? (2 Peter 3:10-12, NKJV)

10 The Day of the Lord will come like a thief, and then with a roar the sky will vanish, the elements will catch fire and melt away, the earth and all that it contains will be burned up. 11 Since everything is coming to an end like this, what holy and saintly lives you should be living 12 while you wait for the Day of God to come, and try to hasten its coming: on that Day the sky will dissolve in flames and the elements melt in the heat. (2 Peter 3:10-12, NJB)

Unlike the localized lake of fire where the corpses of the Beast and False Prophet can be seen, and the same localized one where Satan will be seen, this one is NOT simply localized and will destroy the entire surface of the earth as even the elements will melt and the sky dissolve in flames.

This is an extremely hot fire.

The final fire of 2 Peter 3:10-12 will then be followed by the New Heavens and New Earth (2 Peter 3:13).

A place with no more death nor sorrow (Revelation 21:1-4).

'Gehenna Fire' – 'Never Be Quenched'?

1. Did Jesus speak of UNQUENCHABLE fire in Mark 9:43-48? Was He speaking of Gehenna fire? Notice that the Greek word for 'hell' in verses 43, 45 and 47 is 'Gehenna'.

COMMENT: Jesus repeated five times for EMPHASIS, that this coming Gehenna fire which shall destroy the wicked, would NEVER BE 'QUENCHED'. But the vast majority of people have CARELESSLY ASSUMED that the phrase, "go to hell, into the fire that shall never be quenched" (verse 43), is just one more proof that an eternal, tormenting fiery place for the wicked has been roaring CONTINUOUSLY underground, and will continue forever.

Notice now God's own inspired explanation of UNQUENCHABLE fire.

Christ constantly used the Jerusalem refuse or garbage fire, that burned in the Valley of Hinnom which bordered Jerusalem on the south, to ILLUSTRATE the fire which is to occur at the time of the future purification of the earth's surface.

But was the fire that burned the city refuse QUENCHED in those days? The fires in the Valley of Hinnom kept burning as long as there were bodies of dead people, animals, or refuse, to BURN. THEN THEY NATURALLY WENT OUT! It is important to notice that these fires accomplished their purpose of consuming the dead bodies and refuse, and that it was only AFTER they had accomplished this purpose that they BURNED THEMSELVES OUT. But they never were QUENCHED, or PUT OUT, prematurely by anyone! The flames merely died out when they had nothing more to consume. It could have been said of these fires, "THEY SHALL NOT BE QUENCHED BY ANYONE." They didn't have to be!

So Jesus used the fire in the Valley of Hinnom, which WASN'T QUENCHED by anyone, as a TYPE of the great future worldwide Gehenna fire.

2. Now we'll let the Bible further interpret the MEANING of 'unquenchable fire'. Did God, over 2500 years ago, warn the wicked inhabitants of Jerusalem that He would kindle a fire in Jerusalem's gates which would devour the palaces? Jeremiah 17:27. Did God say this fire "shall NOT BE QUENCHED"?

COMMENT: This fire did occur a few years later and it did DESTROY all the houses of Jerusalem (Jeremiah 52:13). Since God said no person or thing would quench this fire ("it shall not be quenched"), and since it is NOT BURNING TODAY, it obviously went out BY ITSELF after accomplishing its purpose!

3. And now for another example. What PUNISHMENT befell the notorious cities of Sodom and Gomorrah? Genesis 19:24. Was it LITERAL FIRE that destroyed human beings? Luke 17:29. What do we read in Jude 7 about this event? Did they have to "suffer the vengeance of ETERNAL fire"? Is there still a fire burning in those cities which God set aflame long ago and destroyed? OF COURSE NOT!

COMMENT: "ETERNAL fire" means a fire whose results are PERMANENT or everlasting – NOT a fire that BURNS FOREVER! Sodom and Gomorrah have NEVER been rebuilt.

The fires which burned these cities went out of themselves when they CONSUMED ALL COMBUSTIBLE MATERIAL! Clearly none of these scriptures can be used to show that 'fire that shall not be quenched' will torment people forever and ever!

4. Now consider what happens if someone gets a pan and places some paper in it. Then someone lights it with a match or lighter. The paper would then BURN. What HAPPENS to the fire after it consumes the paper? IT GOES OUT on its own! Did anyone need to 'quench' it? No. And consider that only ASHES in the pan would be left.

5. Are the wicked to be reduced to ASHES by the fire which will destroy the earth's surface? Malachi 4:3. How can ASHES be tormented forever and ever? Then the 'wages of sin IS DEATH' by a reduction of the sinner to ashes, and is an eternal – everlasting – punishment, and not an everlasting punishing by torment, isn't it?

COMMENT: Punishing is a continuous action. Punishment has a time limit! Torment will end! God is merciful!

6. Does God promise the righteous a better world after this one is purified by fire? 2 Peter 3:13.

COMMENT: When 2 Peter was written, the Book of Revelation had not been revealed. But the two line up and provide details when looked at together.

In Revelation, the new heaven and new earth are mentioned immediately after the account of the Lake of Fire:

> 1 Now I saw a new heaven and a new earth, for the first heaven and the first earth had passed away. Also there was no more sea. 2 Then I, John, saw the holy city, New Jerusalem, coming down out of heaven from God, prepared as a bride adorned for her husband. 3 And I heard a loud voice from heaven saying, "Behold, the tabernacle of God is with men, and He will dwell with them, and they shall be His people. God Himself will be with them and be their God. (Revelation 21:1-3).

God renews the face of the earth (Psalm 104:30).

God Is Love – and Justice!

The primary reason so many people and human organizations have a FALSE conception of Gehenna fire is that they view the doctrine of hell basically as an ISOLATED doctrine. They FAIL TO UNDERSTAND the OVERALL PURPOSE of God in putting humans on this earth, of offering humans the choice of receiving the gift of eternal life for those who obey Him (cf. Acts 5:32; Hebrews 5:9), or everlasting punishment (not punishing) for disobedience (Malachi 4:1,3).

God created man in His own image and likeness (Genesis 1:26). In the Garden of Eden, He instructed man in the way that would lead to ETERNAL LIFE. Then He told man that doing the WRONG thing – eating of the fruit of the tree which God had forbidden – would lead to DEATH (Genesis 2:17). But Satan, the FATHER of all lies (John 8:44), told the woman, "You will not surely die" (Genesis 3:4). He told her she had an 'immortal soul'! And man has been believing that LIE ever since!

God's purpose is to develop holy, righteous character in man which will make man fit to receive ETERNAL LIFE. God gave ancient Israel His commandments, "that it might be well with them and with their children forever!" (Deuteronomy 5:29).

God's decrees are always for humanity's good. They are not designed as arbitrary decrees which God has set in order to have some excuse for plunging men into flames of fire!

God created humans in His own image in order that humans might develop holy character so God could entrust them with the precious GIFT of ETERNAL LIFE. Notice that God offered Adam and Eve LIFE on one hand, and death on the other.

If an individual rebels against God, is unrepentant and unteachable, then God knows that one would also ABUSE ETERNAL LIFE! If given eternal life while in this SINNING CONDITION, that person would bring misery on him/her and others for all eternity by his/her wrong ways. Certainly the KINDEST THING God could do is NOT give this person eternal life!

God is love (1 John 4:8,16) and all His actions and plans are based on love.

The gift of ETERNAL LIFE for obedience – and the reward of death – ETERNAL DEATH – for disobedience are stressed all through YOUR BIBLE. Only this is consistent with the Scriptures, and with God's plan and purpose – and His character of supreme LOVE! God will not, because of His infinite LOVE, take away anyone's life because of ignorance or weakness, but only if they WILFULLY and KNOWINGLY refuse to obey their Creator.

The warning of Gehenna fire should be a FEARFUL WARNING to those who know God's truth and still stubbornly REFUSE to obey it! It should bring the somber realization that unless we SURRENDER to God's will and His way of love, and refuse to let ANYTHING turn us aside, God will TAKE AWAY forever the life He has given us!

'Worm That Does Not Die'

Many have wondered about a statement found in Mark 9:44, 46 and 48. In these verses of Scripture, Christ spoke of a worm that 'does not die'. Who ever heard of the immortality of worms?!

Some people think that Jesus was referring to PEOPLE as worms and was trying to say that these 'people' never died – but lived on in AGONIZING TORMENT. Those who say this fail to notice that Jesus does not call the wicked 'worms', but instead speaks of THEIR worm, which looks to have literal and allegorical meaning. A similar statement is made in Isaiah 66:24 in which 'their worm' refers to the 'worm' of the 'corpses'. Since it is the 'worm' OF the wicked, then the wicked themselves CANNOT be the 'worms'.

The Lexicons define the Hebrew (Isaiah 66:24) and Greek (Mark 9:44) words translated 'worm' as a grub or MAGGOT.
Christ was not teaching the immortality of people OR worms! Notice what Jesus really meant.

If anything, especially a dead body, landed on a ledge above the garbage fires of 'Gehenna' or even in it, ultimately it could be devoured by many WORMS or MAGGOTS.

It was to these type of worms that Christ was referring when He said, 'their worm does not die'. But Christ didn't mean that each individual worm continued to live forever!

Actually, these maggots come from eggs deposited by flies. Here is the cycle. These eggs give rise to larvae – MAGGOTS – WHICH EAT FLESH and other garbage. They continue in this form a few days, then go through a change called pupation, and finally emerge as flies. THE WORMS DON'T DIE – THEY BECOME FLIES!

These are scientific facts, known by any real student of science. And yet some people think that Christ somehow stated that these larvae continued to live FOREVER in that stage of development! This just goes to show that we should always be careful to use wisdom and common sense in studying God's Word. The Holy Spirit is the spirit of a SOUND MIND (2 Timothy 1:7). Let's rightly use the minds God gave us!

The Greek word which was inspired, and translated into the word 'worm' in Mark 9:44, simply means a grub or maggot, and is a COLLECTIVE expression – like 'fish' or 'deer' or 'sins' or 'corruption' – for worms that devour dead matter, or otherwise destroy the body. These worms do not die, but pupate and become flies. Later, these flies, like all other creatures, WILL return to the dust from which they came. 'ALL are from the dust, and ALL return to dust' (Ecclesiastes 3:20).

As mentioned before, in Isaiah 66:24, we again find that the inspired word simply means a common grub or a maggot. These worms or larvae also feed on the dead bodies for a few days, and then emerge as flies. Thus, these worms 'do not die' but continue to develop into flies just as any normal, healthy maggot! The flies continue to deposit their eggs ONLY AS LONG AS there are dead bodies or other matter for the larvae to feed on.

Isaiah 66:24 specifically points to the fact that others will be able to see what happened to those that transgressed against God. Hence allegorically, their corruption/worm will be historically known—in that sense it also does not die.

Furthermore, we realize that worms do not have immortal souls as Ecclesiastes 3:19 shows that NO LIVING CREATURE IS born with an immortal soul (see also 1 Corinthians 15:53-54; 1 Timothy 6:16).

The Bible is one book that makes GOOD SENSE! So let us always carefully study these perplexing scriptures through, and not jump to our own conclusions.

Let's live by God's Word so we may receive the GIFT of eternal life, and not the wages of sin which is death (Romans 6:23). This death will come by a fire which God will not permit to be quenched – BUT WILL BURN ITSELF OUT by consuming this earth's surface, and all of the wicked who will then become nothing but ashes (Malachi 4:1).

If we will HONESTLY search the scriptures and LIVE by them, we will most certainly inherit eternal life.

Lazarus and the Rich Man

Jesus' PARABLE of Lazarus and the rich man (Luke 16:19-31) is perhaps one of the most – if not THE most – outstanding texts used by those who seek to prove there is a fiery hell in which the wicked are suffering excruciating torture today.

Exactly what did Jesus intend to illustrate by this PARABLE? Let's get the facts straight!

1. Did Lazarus – a poor but RIGHTEOUS beggar mentioned in this parable – DIE? Luke 16:22. Was he carried by angels to 'Abraham's bosom'?

COMMENT: God gave Abraham and his 'seed' the promise of the earth for an eternal inheritance. If we are Christ's, we are considered by God as Abraham's seed – children – and are thus also heirs with Abraham to receive this promise (Galatians 3:29). Through FAITH we may all become 'CHILDREN OF ABRAHAM' (Galatians 3:7). This is an INTIMATE RELATIONSHIP – a close or bosom relationship – to Abraham. We are to be in CLOSE CONTACT with him in SHARING this promise. It is like being TAKEN TO ABRAHAM'S BOSOM (Luke 16:22). And so RIGHTEOUS Lazarus was taken to Abraham's bosom in this parable.

When, then, did Abraham actually receive these promises? The startling answer of Scripture is – HE DIDN'T! – HE HAS NOT, EVEN YET IN OUR DAY, INHERITED THESE PROMISES!

We learned in Lesson 13 (BNP Magazine Apr-Jun 2018) that Abraham will inherit the promises at the RESURRECTION of the just, when Christ returns to establish the Kingdom of God on earth.

And what about Lazarus, the beggar of Jesus' parable? He, being intimately RELATED to Abraham, SPIRITUALLY SPEAKING, will also receive the promises when he is resurrected at that same time! Lazarus is a type of Abraham's children who are to receive the promises at the resurrection.

2. But what about the SINFUL rich man of Jesus' parable? Did he also DIE? Luke 16:22. And is the next picture we see of him one where he is lifting his eyes from the GRAVE – not from a fiery place of eternal torment – but the GRAVE, and calling to the resurrected Abraham for a FEW DROPS of water to COOL ONLY HIS TONGUE, being in MENTAL torment? Luke 16:23-24. How could he lift up his eyes UNLESS HE WERE RESURRECTED?

COMMENT: The word 'hell' used here is translated from the original Greek word HADES, which you know means the 'grave'. It is NOT from the Greek word GEHENNA, which helps represent the future lake of fire that will destroy the wicked forever. The rich man, at this moment, is pictured as COMING UP OUT

OF HIS GRAVE through a resurrection.

When Christ comes, the righteous will be resurrected to immortality, and Christ will say, "Come, you blessed [who are here Abraham and the beggar] ... INHERIT the kingdom prepared for you..." (Matthew 25:31-34). Abraham and Lazarus will have ESCAPED, through the sacrifice of Christ, the judgment of eternal death by Gehenna fire — they will have been IMMORTAL FOR OVER 1000 YEARS BEFORE this rich man is resurrected to be burned in the lake of fire (Revelation 20:15). Until then, he has been dead in the grave having NO RECOLLECTION of the passing of time (Ecclesiastes 9:5). But at his resurrection from the grave, the rich man sees the flames of the lake of fire surrounding him, which he KNOWS will DESTROY HIM FOREVER. Being in great MENTAL agony, he asks for just a LITTLE water to cool his tongue which has become dry from his MENTAL ANGUISH. He does not ask for BUCKETS FULL of water to put the fire out. An IMPOSSIBILITY, he knows.

3. What will Abraham then answer the rich man? Luke 16:25-26.

COMMENT: The great GULF between the two will be the DIFFERENCE between mortality and immortality. Those who are made immortal shall never die because they will be born of God (Revelation 20:6). Abraham and the beggar will be on the IMMORTAL side of this gulf — the MORTAL unrighteous rich man on the OTHER, facing eternal death by fire.

And many of the condemned will, like the rich man, want their relatives warned, not knowing that all will ALREADY have had their chance to be saved (Luke 16:27, 28).

How clear that the PARABLE of 'Lazarus and the Rich Man' DOES NOT PROVE ETERNAL PUNISHING by God! Rather, by this parable, Christ was preaching the GOOD NEWS of SALVATION!! He was picturing the RESURRECTION TO ETERNAL LIFE and the inheritance of the Kingdom of God on this earth forever.

Christ was also picturing the alternative of eternal life — ETERNAL DEATH IN THE LAKE OF FIRE — If we don't accept the GOOD NEWS of how we may be saved, and ACT upon it!

What Does PENTECOST MEAN to You?

By Herbert W. Armstrong

This is an extract from article was originally published by the old Worldwide Church of God in the May 1979 edition of its old Good News magazine.

Bible References in this article are from the King James Version.

This Feast of Firstfruits corrects the most universally believed false doctrine in Christianity! What is the TRUTH?

Do you KNOW what is the most universally believed false doctrine in the Christian world? God's annual Sabbaths were given to keep the true Church in the true knowledge of our Maker's master plan.

The one original, yet persecuted Church of God, stands alone in keeping these annual festivals. And it alone has that basic UNDERSTANDING.

That universally believed false doctrine is that all humanity is LOST — consigned to an eternally burning hell — unless they 'get saved' by accepting Jesus Christ as personal Savior NOW! They say that we, NOW, are in the ONLY day of salvation that when Christ returns to earth the door to salvation will be CLOSED! Unless you are 'saved' NOW, you are LOST!

Just last night I heard the world's most famous evangelist tell a massive audience (on television) that we, now, are in the ONLY day of salvation — that tomorrow may be too late. Many are frightened into 'making their decision for Christ'.

That false belief implies that when Jesus Christ returns in supreme POWER and GLORY, He will be helpless to save you! On the contrary God's Word says Jesus is coming, 1) to restore the government of God, setting up the KINGDOM OF GOD, and 2) to call ALL people still living to salvation and eternal life.

What is the TRUTH?

What, then, is the TRUTH that the Feast of Firstfruits is given to teach us?

It teaches us the very opposite of what this world's 'Christianity' believes.

It teaches us that we of the TRUE Church are the 'FIRSTFRUITS' ONLY — the FIRST to receive salvation through Christ. It teaches us that all others are NOT YET CALLED. It teaches us that as Jesus said, "NO MAN CAN come to me, except the Father which hath sent me draw him" (John 6:44).

But isn't God the Father desperately trying to draw all humans NOW? Emphatically no! — not yet! Was God unjust? No! Never!

Notice what God did, right after our first parents rejected God as their RULER , their Revealer of knowledge and as their Savior with the gift of everlasting life.

'And the Eternal God said, "Behold, the man is become as one of us, to know good and evil: and now, lest he put forth his hand, and take also of the tree of life, and eat, and live for ever." Therefore the Eternal God sent him forth from the garden of Eden, to till the ground from whence he was taken. So he drove out the man; and placed cherubim at the east of the garden of Eden, and a flaming sword which turned every way, to keep the way of the tree of life' (Gen. 3:22-24).

Thus, ALL MANKIND was BARRED from access to God or receiving eternal life — all but the comparative FEW God would specially call for some performance leading to the Kingdom of God.

In effect, God said to MANKIND through Adam and Eve: 'You have made your own decision. You have rejected me as your God and your Ruler, Revealer of knowledge and Savior. Therefore I have cut you and the whole world that will spring from you off from all contact with me. Go and form your own governments, your own religions, your own production and dissemination of knowledge. However, I shall reserve the prerogative to specially call into my service such as I shall choose, for a part in preparing for the Kingdom of God. Otherwise, the world that will develop from you is CUT OFF from all contact with me for 6,000 years, when the Kingdom of God shall be established, ruling ALL NATIONS!'

Far from trying to get every human saved spiritually during the 6,000 years, God CUT OFF all humanity — save the comparative FEW He would specially call.

THAT IS WHY Jesus said, "No man can come to me" during this 6,000 year period, except God the Father specially calls them — and He has called this few not just for salvation, but for a special service preparing for the Kingdom of God, as well.

After that 6,000 years expires, Christ will come again to earth, this time in SUPREME POWER AND GLORY, to set up GOD'S GOVERNMENT. Satan shall be banished. Then, during the seventh thousand years, God will call EVERYBODY then living.

And after the seventh millennium, God will resurrect to mortal life all the billions of people who had not been called for spiritual salvation.

Is God discriminating?

Those who have been called have had to overcome Satan. Those called later shall not.

WHY this difference? We might reason: Is God discriminating against us, who have to resist and overcome Satan, when all converted during the millennium will not? But there is no injustice with God.

Yet there is a DIFFERENCE!

THINK ON THIS! God is calling ONLY a comparative FEW now. Is that an evil or a blessing? It is a tremendous blessing, for, referring to God's Church for this Church dispensation ONLY, Jesus says: "And he that overcometh [overcomes Satan and self and the world], and keepeth my works unto the end, to him will I give power over the nations: And he shall rule them with a rod of iron..." (Rev. 2:26-27), and, "To him that overcometh [Satan, the world and self] will I grant to sit with me in my throne " (Rev. 3:21).

Those promises pertain only to those called before Christ's return. So some wanting to accuse God might ask, "Isn't this UNFAIR to those not called NOW? They have no chance to know, now, the joys of God's Holy Spirit. And they have no promise of exalted position or power when they are 'saved' later!"

Absolutely NO! There is no injustice with God. I'm sure those NOT now called do not feel they are discriminated against. They don't want to be called. And as for high and glorified position, that is a responsibility, and I do not know of anyone uncalled who has any sense whatever of dissatisfaction because he may not have such exalted position in the world TOMORROW, ruled by the Kingdom of God.

But nevertheless, this is an interesting point. Those called now do have Satan, Satan's world and their own human nature to overcome — and that requires effort, self-denial and willpower, which most humans would not want to pay.

But what about those who shall be called for the first time, and converted, after Christ returns? Shall they not have any opportunity to inherit a high and lofty position?

Probably the highest and most lofty positions in both Church and State in the world to come already have been allotted.

We know that each of the original 12 apostles will be ruler over one of the 12 nations springing from the 12 tribes of Israel. We know that David will be king over them and those under them. We may well assume that Abraham will have even a higher position. Those are not only the highest honors — they are likewise the highest and most demanding responsibilities.

Probably the chief seats of authority in the world tomorrow ruled by the KINGDOM OF GOD will be already filled at Christ's coming. But, during the thousand years, population (human) will increase and new positions in government and in spiritual administration will increase. Also, in the Great White Throne Judgment later.

Called to more than salvation

But for us now, it is imperative that we understand that those CALLED and inducted by God into His Church NOW, have been called for MORE THAN JUST SPIRITUAL SALVATION AND THE GIFT OF ETERNAL LIFE. We are called, every one of us, for a PART in preparing for the Kingdom of God!

For our part now, in this present 'Philadelphia era', each of you is called for the mission of loyally backing up the GREAT COMMISSION of proclaiming the true Gospel to the whole world — and one important thing more: When Jesus comes to RULE, His Wife THE CHURCH will have made herself ready — to be holy and without blemish, not having spot or wrinkle or any such thing. And we in the Church as a whole HAVE NOT ATTAINED FULLY TO THAT HOLY STATURE AS YET.

And our work is not finished until we do allow God to bring us unitedly to that state — ready to leave this world of flesh and blood — and to enter an entirely NEW WORLD — the Church made immortal, composed of SPIRIT! Our job to which God has called us is far from finished!

In this connection, I have been thinking recently and coming to understand better WHY God brought me back to life, after both heart and breathing had totally ceased. If mouth-to-mouth resuscitation had not been successfully employed, I would have remained totally unconscious until the resurrection.

Incidentally, regardless of number of days or years till the resurrection, it would have seemed the next second to me. ...

As we come to God's Feast of Firstfruits (Pentecost), let us bear forcibly in mind we in God's Church must be MADE READY — for Christ is coming SOON — and we are NOT YET FULLY READY to be instantly changed and caught up to meet our Lord as He comes in clouds!

In 2019, Pentecost runs from sunset June 8th to sunset June 9th.

For more on God's calling, check out the free online booklet: Is God Calling You? available at ccog.org

OMENS? DIVINATION? HOROSCOPES? THE ORIGIN OF ASTROLOGY

By Scott G Rockhold

This article was originally published in the November 1976 edition of the old Worldwide Church of God who originally held the copyright.

Polls show that millions of Americans firmly believe that astrology works. But most have no idea how this ancient practice actually began. Read here the eye-opening account of the origin of astrology.

Astrological Signs

Slowly the aged, white-haired Chaldean priest raised the long, sharp knife above his head. He paused for a moment, reverently addressing a prayer to the sun god Shamash, then swiftly plunged the blade deep into the belly of the young sheep tied across the temple altar. Blood spurted from the incision as the priest, assisted by junior temple officials, deftly slit the animal open. The priests expertly examined the now steaming liver, lungs, and intestines of the sheep. Suddenly the elderly chief priest gasped with fear and surprise as he saw a long yellowish mark on one side of the liver — a certain sign of coming destruction.

Hastily, the old priest scurried out of the temple and called for his assistants to prepare a boat for the trip up the Euphrates to Babylon. He had to warn the king at once not to campaign against the Elamites in the east this year. The great gods had spoken through the body of the sheep — the abnormal mark on the liver meant the king and his army were certain to meet disaster!

Babylonian Divination

Ceremonies similar to the one described above were carried out thousands upon thousands of times during the history of ancient Babylonia and Assyria, located in what is now modern Iraq. As their religious documents and inscriptions clearly show, the Babylonians firmly believed that powerful gods communicated with man through all kinds of natural events and conditions — the markings on the entrails of a sacrificial animal, the behavior of animals or humans in the streets, the shape of a miscarried fetus, the pattern formed by smoke from an oil lamp or by water poured on oil, and, not least, the positions of planets and stars in the sky.

Such events, believed to be messages of the future, are called omens, and the art of seeking and interpreting omens is called divination. Ancient societies believed omens were messages from the gods revealing future events. Many peoples of the ancient world — the Babylonians, Assyrians, Egyptians, Greeks, and Romans — practiced divination.

Probably the most popular form of divination in ancient Babylon was the examination of the entrails of animals, especially sheep, that were sacrificed to the god. Just before slaying the animal, the divination priest beseeched the gods to write his message on the entrails of the sheep. When the organs were examined, any unusual marks, lumps, or shapes were interpreted as the god's answer; even the normal configuration of the organs had significance. Hundreds of clay tablets have been unearthed from the lands of Babylonia and Assyria bearing detailed instructions to the priests on how to interpret the marks on entrails of sacrificial animals as well as how to interpret thousands of other ominous events and conditions. Such practices were known far and wide; the Bible even records that Nebuchadnezzar of Babylon 'looked in the liver' for guidance from the gods in his campaigns against Judah (Ezekiel 21:21).

The Stars and Planets

As the Babylonian creation myth, the Enuma Elish, clearly shows, the stars and planets were believed to be the signs of the most powerful gods, and in some cases were actually gods themselves.

Naturally, since the stars and planets were viewed as divine, or symbols of divine action and power, they became the objects of careful observation by the divination priests. Eventually, detailed records of the movements and positions of the planets were kept. These records and calculations based upon them became the foundation for not only astronomy, but astrology as well.

Because the Babylonians and Assyrians believed the heavenly bodies were representative of the gods, their positions and movements were obviously of great significance to life and events on earth. We know that by about 700 B.C., the planets, including the sun and moon, were being carefully watched by the Assyrians for their impact on the life of the king. Numerous letters and state records tell us of warnings by the priests for the king to be careful, or to have rituals carried out to attempt to avoid the predicted disaster.

Other astronomical omens were favorable to the king but unfavorable to foreigners. Langers' Encyclopedia of World History shows that the earliest development of astrology was associated with Babylonian magic and divination:

> The most characteristic and influential features of Babylonian religion, aside from its mythology, were the elaborate systems of magical practices (incantations) and the interpretation of omens (divination), particularly the movements and position of the heavenly bodies (astrology), the actions of animals, and the characteristics of the liver of sacrificial victims (p.26).

The Zodiac

The Babylonians were also the inventors of the zodiac. Their astronomers divided the heavens into sections in order to tell time at night as well as seasons of the year. At first there were some 36 sections or areas, corresponding to various stars or constellations. Later this number was reduced to 12, or one constellation for each month of the year.

Some of the Babylonian constellations or 'signs' bore the same names as they do today. Thus the Babylonian 'bull of Anu' is the constellation (or sign) Taurus; 'the Great Twins' are the constellation Gemini; 'the lion' Leo; 'the Scorpion' is naturally Scorpio. Other signs, however, were given different names by Greek astrologers some centuries later; the 'modern' names for the signs of the zodiac arc actually Greek or Latin.

Most, if not all, of the constellations of the Babylonian zodiac were mythological figures which we read about in the great Babylonian myths and epics. For instance the 'bull of Anu' was sent by the goddess Ishtar to punish the hero Gilgamesh. The planets and the stars as well were considered divine beings: the god Shamash was the sun, the planet Venus (Babylonian Dilbat) was the 'star' of the goddess Ishtar.

By about 450 B.C., the planets, stars, and zodiac were all put together into one cosmic system of the gods that supposedly controlled or influenced an individual's life here on earth.

The First Horoscopes

Not coincidentally, it is just about this time that we have the first known horoscopes. These horoscopes, found inscribed on clay tablets in Babylonian cuneiform characters, were cast at the moment of birth, just as modern horoscopes are cast. And like modern horoscopes, they tell the exact positions of the planets in the zodiac and how they will influence the life of the newborn individual.

The first known horoscope dates to the year 410 B.C. It is found on a clay tablet now kept at Oxford University. It reads:

Month Nisan, night of the 14th... son of Shumausur, son of Shuma-iddina, descendant of Deke, was born. At that time the moon was below the Horn of the Scorpion. Jupiter in Pisces, Venus in Taurus, Saturn in Cancer, Mars in Gemini; Mercury, which had set for the last time was still invisible... Things will be good for you (Journal of Cuneiform Studies, 1952, p. 54).

Several other horoscopes, quite similar in form to this one, are known from about the same time. It is plain from these records that astrological horoscopes, applied to human individuals at birth, were a Babylonian invention.

The Greek Connection

By about 400 B.C., Greek scientists and philosophers were traveling throughout the Mediterranean world. Especially during and after the time of Alexander the Great, the Greeks began to learn of the beliefs and science of the Babylonians, Egyptians, and others. With the help of the Babylonian priest Berossus, whose treatise on astrology reached Greece about 250 B.C., they took over and modified the Babylonian system of astrology. The Greeks even kept many of the names for the astrological signs; to others they gave new names. However, it was clearly recognized that the astrological predictions and interpretations were still based on pagan Babylonian mythology.

In the first century B.C., the Greek historian Diodorus wrote the following about the astrology of the Chaldeans:

> Under the course in which the planets move are situated, according to them, thirty stars, which they designate as 'counselling gods'; of these, one half oversee the regions above the earth and the other half those beneath the earth, having under their purview the affairs of mankind and likewise those of the heavens.... Twelve of these gods, they say, hold chief authority, and to each of these the Chaldeans assign a month and one of the sign of the zodiac, as they are called. And through the midst of these signs, they say, both the sun and moon and the five planets make their course... (Diodorus, II, 30, 30).

The Greek astrologers greatly modified and embellished the astrological system that the Chaldean divination priests had devised. They organized astrological methods into a complex scheme of houses, aspects, signs, and planets, with dozens, if not hundreds, of rules and variations.

The greatest of the Greek astrologers was the Alexandrian astronomer and mathematican Claudius Ptolemy. His astrological work, The Tetrabiblos, became the handbook upon which all subsequent astrology is based. However, even in this 'scientific' work, important traces of Babylonian and Greek mythology appear. Notice Ptolemy's comments on the influence of the planet Mars (in Greek and Roman mythology the god of war):

> Mars... brings about wars, civil faction, capture, enslavement, uprising, the wrath of leaders, and sudden deaths arising from such cases... (Tetrabiblos, II, 8).

While many of Ptolemy's interpretations of the heavens stem from the (mistaken) astronomical beliefs of his day, it is clear that much of his astrology is ultimately based on pagan mythology, which in many respects goes back to the myths and beliefs of ancient Babylon. Furthermore, the elaborate astrological system worked out by Ptolemy actually forms the basis of much of modern astrology.

This then is the origin of a practice followed by millions of ... devotees. Regardless of whether one actually believes in astrology or not, it is clear that such beliefs ultimately originated in the magic and superstition of the divination priests of ancient Babylonia and Assyria.

Editor: Perhaps it should be added that in the 21st century, the astrological signs in the heavens do NOT even correlate to the dates that people believe. For example, those born between March 21 and April 19 are considered to have Aries as their astrological sign. While different thousands over years ago, the sun is no longer within the constellation of Aries during much of that period. From March 11 to April 18, the sun is actually in the constellation of Pisces.

The following is based on the sun's current

path, and compares it to the dates still used by astrologers (which are shown in parentheses):

Capricorn — Jan. 20 to Feb. 16 (Dec. 23 to Jan. 21)
Aquarius — Feb. 16 to March 11 (Jan. 22 to Feb. 20)
Pisces — March 11 to April 18 (Feb. 21 to March 19)
Aries — April 18 to May 13 (March 20 to April 20)
Taurus — May 13 to June 21 (April 21 to May 21)
Gemini — June 21 to July 20 (May 22 to June 22)
Cancer — July 20 to Aug. 10 (June 23 to July 22)
Leo — August 10 to Sept. 16 (July 23 to Aug. 22)
Virgo — Sept. 16 to Oct. 30 (Aug. 23 to Sept. 22)
Libra — Oct. 30 to Nov. 23 (Sept. 23 to Oct. 22)
Scorpio — Nov. 23 to Nov. 29 (Oct. 23 to Nov. 22)
Ophiuchus — Nov. 29 to Dec. 17 (not included in the Zodiac)
Sagittarius — Dec. 17 to Jan. 20 (Nov. 23 to Dec. 22)

(Braganca P. Astrology: Why Your Zodiac Sign and Horoscope Are Wrong. Live Science, September 20, 2017).

Thus, most people were not born under the sign that astrologers claim. Hence, the supposed characteristics of one 'born under a sign' are actually supposed to be related to another sign. Therefore, this is another reason to discount astrology.

Youth & Singles: Q&A

Q. My parents don't like the guy I'm dating and are trying to split us up. Why don't they want me to have fun and be happy?

A. If your parents disapprove of your friend, be cautious! Your parents probably do want you to be happy. They have likely seen similar situations - perhaps in their own experience - where someone has been deeply hurt, and they don't want that to happen to you.

Realize that your parents know you better in many ways than you know yourself. Also realize that they were once teens themselves. They've seen more of the trap doors and problems of life than you have.

Consider their advice seriously. Talk to them calmly when both you and they have the time. Ask them to explain why they do not care for your friend. If you will listen to them, you might be able to learn a bit more about yourself, and about your friend. And you can avoid the heartaches many have reaped because they ignore what can be the best source of personal dating advice available outside of the Bible – decent parents!

Q. Many of my friends are engaging in sexting. That's okay, right?

A. While we realize that many teens engage in sexting, and some 'authorities' claim that this is a good thing (e.g. Teen sexting may be more common than you think. Reuters, February 27, 2018), no it is not.

Sexting is essentially a form of lust-inciting pornography and is not appropriate (cf. 1 Timothy 2:9; Matthew 5:28).

For those who are unfamiliar with the term, sexting is sending, receiving, or forwarding sexually explicit messages, photographs or images, primarily between mobile phones and/or other electronic devices.

Do not 'date' by, nor with, sexting.

Furthermore, realize that although many think that sexting is 'cute', if you engage in this there can be images of you in ways you do not want everyone to see for a very long time.

Sexting is wrong and the consequences are not worth it.

We are open to covering other questions that are not in our booklet as well. If you have appropriate questions that you would like answered here, you can send them to the Continuing Church of God at the address shown in the front of this magazine or send an email for consideration.

April - June 2019

Made in the USA
San Bernardino, CA
22 February 2019